# A STUDY IN TROOP FRONTAGE

---
Monograph No. 4
---

Prepared in the
Historical Branch, War Plans Division
General Staff

December, 1919

WASHINGTON
GOVERNMENT PRINTING OFFICE
1920

In the interest of creating a more extensive selection of rare historical book reprints, we have chosen to reproduce this title even though it may possibly have occasional imperfections such as missing and blurred pages, missing text, poor pictures, markings, dark backgrounds and other reproduction issues beyond our control. Because this work is culturally important, we have made it available as a part of our commitment to protecting, preserving and promoting the world's literature. Thank you for your understanding.

UG444
U6

War Department.
Document No. 992.
*Office of The Adjutant General.*

WAR DEPARTMENT,
WASHINGTON, *December 19, 1919.*

The following publication, entitled "A Study in Troop Frontage," prepared in the Historical Branch, War Plans Division, General Staff, is approved and published for the information and guidance of all concerned.

[062.1, A. G. O.]

BY ORDER OF THE SECRETARY OF WAR:

PEYTON C. MARCH,
*General, Chief of Staff.*

OFFICIAL:
P. C. HARRIS,
*The Adjutant General.*

# A STUDY IN TROOP FRONTAGE.

**1. Introduction.**

The war with Germany showed the same essential characteristics as previous wars. There is a possibility that the degeneration of the war on the western front into trench warfare was not inevitable, and that the whole war might have been fought out as an open-warfare problem. However, by the late fall of 1914 the western front had stabilized and trench warfare was developing.(1) From this time, the outstanding feature of the war, which continued to be a governing feature during its continuance, was the existence of a continuous western battle front, necessitating frontal attacks. This factor restricted the art of maneuver to the massing of troops on various parts of the front.(2) For this reason a study of the strength in which various parts of the front were held or attacked is not only interesting from a historical viewpoint, but valuable in deducing sound practices for future use.

Features of the War. Haig, p. 1, W. D. D. 952, 1919.
Deductions from the World War. Von Freytag-Loringhoven, p. 129.
The War of Positions. Azan. (1)

Features of the War. Haig, pp. 6, 7. (2)

Even an estimation of the number of troops to the yard in battle is attended with considerable difficulty and a good deal of uncertainty.(3) The documents available are so incomplete and liable to error that to base any general conclusions on facts drawn from the documents in individual instances would be dangerous, and might be misleading. There are, at present, available documents sufficiently well authenticated to guarantee obtaining approximately correct figures for the practice of the employment of American troops in France. However, it must be realized that even the most reliable documents do not invariably present the facts as they existed. Men get lost or skulk, and are not actually present on the battle line as active riflemen, although they may be carried as present for duty on division returns. As for publications pertaining to armies other than the American Army, they must be viewed with considerable distrust. It was perfectly natural that during the war both French and British military authorities should keep secret the real strength and disposition of forces. As instancing the

Memorandum on Number of Troops to the Yard in the Principal Battles since 1850, p. 1. U. 167-G 74. General Staff College Library. (3)

difficulty of obtaining facts, it may be noted that the only available figures on the organization of British divisions place the infantry rifle strength at approximately 12,000 rifles in twelve battalions.(4) The only document indicating that the actual organization had fallen below this strength is a cablegram from Gen. Pershing in January, 1918, which indicates a contemplated reduction of British divisions from twelve to nine battalions.(5) However, it is a fact, attested to by American officers serving with the British, that this reduction was actually made by the early spring of 1918, before the German offensive of March 21, 1918, and that even the nine remaining battalions were seldom maintained at full strength. During the campaign of 1918, when the 27th and 30th Divisions of the Second Corps were considerably under strength, it was estimated that each one of these divisions had an effective rifle strength twice that of the normal British division with which they were operating.(6) It is, nevertheless, believed that, from a general study of conditions existing and the disposition of forces taken to meet these conditions, approximate figures can be obtained and valuable lessons learned.

*Margin notes:* Strength and Organization of the Armies of France, etc. W.D.D.22, General Staff College Library. Changes in Organization Found Necessary during Progress of European War. W. C. D. 4886-23. General Staff College Library. (4) Confidential cablegram 487, A. E. F., Jan. 13, 1918. H. B. files. (5) Statement of Brig. Gen. Geo. Simonds, Chief of Staff, 2d Corps, Nov. 8, 1919. (6)

### 2. Bases for Computation.

In a study involving comparisons in such a large field as the war with Germany offers, a basis of comparison must be immediately established and consistently adhered to, in order to avoid confusion in the mind of the student and consequent lack of clearness. For the purpose of this study one hundred yards is taken as the frontage unit, and the strength is expressed in the number of Infantry rifles.

The choice of hundreds of yards instead of kilometers is unimportant. The yard is our national and traditionally our military unit. It was used throughout the war by the British.(7) While the A. E. F. in France used the French unit as convenient, the units are easily convertible.(8) (100 yards equal 91.44 meters, roughly, 1/11 of a kilometer.) The number one hundred in yards is taken to obviate the use of decimals in number of rifles per unit of front. In this connection it should be noted that the width of front given in the following paragraphs is measured from the actual front line as it appears on operation maps. Following in general the eccentricities of that line, it may vary therefore very greatly from

*Margin notes:* British situation maps D-1. Map room files, G-3, A. E. F. (7) Report of C. in C., A. E. F., cabled Nov. 20, 1918, pp. 10 and 19. (8)

the width of the zone in which the unit concerned is employed, the width of the zone being normally measured at right angles to the direction of expected attack or resistance.

The choice of the Infantry rifle as the unit of strength is not so easily justified. The proportion of tanks, airplanes, special weapons, and above all, artillery, entered largely into the strength in which fronts were held or attacked.(9) However, principal authorities agree on the supreme importance of the rifle and the fact that rifle strength is a true index of effective man power. Accepting rifle strength as an index, it must be consistently arrived at.(10) Here it is taken as Infantry rifles in divisions which are in the front line as units and dispose wholly of their Infantry. The division is the unit universally used in computing strength.(11) It is the responsible unit in both attack and defense,(12) combining as it does, all major arms except the Air Service, and if employed as a complete division must have at its disposition all Infantry rifles. The Infantry rifles only are included in computing frontage strength. The regiments of divisional engineers are powerful organizations, armed with the rifle. They were frequently used as Infantry.(13) However, such use is not contemplated in the organization of divisions, nor was it invariable or even customary.(14) The British division had a similar powerful engineer organization.(15) The French, however, allowed the division only the engineers necessary for purely engineering work.(16) To include the engineers in figuring frontage strength would complicate, without increasing the value of, the figures arrived at. The American Infantry rifle strength as included in the four Infantry regiments of the division is 13,568.(17) This includes the automatic rifle strength, but excludes the machine-gun strength. An effort was made throughout to keep divisions up to strength by replacements,(18) and they can be accepted as being at approximately full strength, except where otherwise noted. At the beginning of the war the British Infantry division, with a total of some 18,000, was considered to dispose of 11,676 Infantry rifles.(19) It is impossible from the facts at hand to determine exactly how this strength varied during the war, but in January, 1918, it had apparently dropped to something like 9,000.(20) Following heavy losses in the

Features of the War. Haig, pp. 17-25. (9)
Id., p. 13.
Rept. of C. in C., A. E. F., cabled Nov. 20, 1918, p. 3.
The War with Germany. Ayers, p. 104. (10)
Rept. of C. in C., A. E. F., cabled Nov. 20, 1918, p. 3.
The War with Germany. Ayers, p. 101. (11)
Instructions on the Offensive Action of Large Units in Battle, No. 767, Headquarters, A. E. F., 1918.
Instructions on the Defensive Action of Large Units in Battle. W. D. D. 794, 1918.
T. of O., Series A, 1918. (12)
F. O. 49, 1st Div., Oct. 8, 1918. H. B. 201-13. (13)
Appendix to par. 3, F. O. 47, 1st Div., Oct. 3, 1918. H. B. 201-13. (14)
Changes in Organization Found Necessary during Progress of European War. W.C.D. 4886-23. General Staff College Library. (15)
Tableaux d'Effectifs, 1913-1918. General Staff College Library. (16)
T. of O., Series A, 1918. Tables 1 and 3. (17)
Rept. of C. in C., A. E. F. cabled Nov. 20, 1918, p. 23. (18)
Strength and Organization of the Armies of France, etc. W. C. D. No. 22. General Staff College Library. (19)

German offensives of March 21 and April 11, 1918, this strength was undoubtedly further reduced and by the summer of 1918 can be taken as approximately 6,000.(21) A normal French division in 1914 included 4 Infantry regiments of 12 battalions, with 1,000 Infantry rifles to the battalion.(22) This organization was also modified during the war, and at the time of the American entry in force in 1918 the normal French Infantry division included 1 Infantry brigade of 3 regiments and had an Infantry rifle strength of 6,880, exclusive of the machine-gun companies.(23) The reduction in rifle strength in the division would naturally be gradual. It was recognized and accepted as inevitable, however, by the change in organization made in 1916, after great losses had been suffered at Verdun, but before the battle on the Somme.(24) The strength of Infantry in French Infantry divisions is given by Gen. Pershing in May, 1918, as being one-half that of the Infantry strength in an American division.(25) This would make the Infantry rifle strength of a French division from that date approximately 6,750.

With the factors of strength and unit of front established, there remains necessary a classification of various types of front in order to study the strength in which they were held or attacked. In a war which passed from open warfare through the most stilted form of trench fighting and approached absolutely open warfare again in the days preceding the armistice, types run into one another. The division into four types is therefore arbitrary. These types are: (a) The quiet front; (b) the active front; (c) the front of a major operation on a stabilized line; (d) the front in open warfare. This classification is more natural in the character of the war after the American entry than in the trench warfare which preceded it. However, the last year of the war is the most fruitful part for the purposes of this study. From the German offensive of March 21, 1918, the part played by the man with the rifle on the western front became increasingly important.(26) In spite of the immense number of participants and casualties at Verdun and on the Somme, these operations were in principle a conflict of material resources, artillery, ammunition and trench mechanisms and were not essentially based on the rifle strength per yard.(27)

(a) A quiet front is taken as one on which the character of the ground or the disposition of forces renders it unlikely that a major operation will develop. (b) An active front is taken as one on which active major operations have recently occurred, or on which they can be expected soon to occur. (c) The front of a major operation on a stabilized line is one on which a major operation on such a line is actually in progress and is restricted to the center of attack or defense in which participation is complete. (d) The front in open warfare is one on which action is concerned with an enemy in the open and not with a continuous line held by or against the enemy.

### 3. General Discussion of Formations.

Before citing instances from which to draw frontage strength, it is interesting to note in general formations adopted in attack and in defense and in particular those adopted by American divisions. It must not, however, be forgotten that whatever the formation, a division must be considered to engage on its front its entire rifle strength present within the division.

The French formation for attack in 1914 may be accepted as not abnormal. Briefly, it employed depth with only the necessary troops deployed.(28) On the defensive an attempt to preserve depth was evident in the organization of positions into trench systems in the earlier years of trench warfare. An even distribution in depth, however, was sacrificed to the desirability of utilizing the shelter afforded by trenches for the protection of all troops. This tended toward a dense occupation of trenches which was emphasized at points of tactical importance.(29) These methods proved too costly at Verdun and on the Somme,(30) and were abandoned in favor of very deep formations to conserve man power and to give elasticity to the defense. In attack, depth formations were habitual.(31) No authenticated instance is known of deliberate use of mass formations. Periodic reports in the press of all nations of enemy attacks in mass probably record honest delusions. The impression of power received on the front of a battalion advancing in an attack maneuver is tremendous, even though the battalion be organized more than 600 yards in depth. The human mind in such cases tends to associate mass with power.

London Times History of the War. Vol. I, p. 73. (28)

The War of Positions. Azan, p. 38 et seq. (29)

History of the World War. Simonds. Vol. III. (30)

Instruction on the Offensive Use of Large Units in Battle. No. 767. Hq. A. E. F., 1918.
Instructions on the Defensive Use of Large Units in Battle. W. D. D. 794, 1918. (31)

A depth formation was habitually used by American divisions. The exact formation, however, depended on the physical and military aspect of the front and the established practice in the division in question. One experienced division held or attacked with brigades abreast, regiments abreast, battalions in depth, as a normal formation.(32) Another varied its formations and sometimes attacked with brigades in depth.(33) At times on very quiet fronts divisions were compelled to hold with reduced depth.

### 4. American Occupation of a Quiet Front.

On August 19, 1918, the 5th Division held a front of about 325 hundred yards in the St. Die Sector.(34) Its Infantry rifle strength on this date was about 12,000. (35) The frontage strength per hundred yards was therefore about 37 Infantry rifles. The St. Die Sector was in the heart of the Vosges Mountains, whose physical characteristics were unfavorable to major operations. At this period major operations were in progress or contemplated from the Moselle to the sea, and quiet fronts would naturally be lightly held.(36)

On July 26, 1918, the 77th Division held a front of about 185 hundred yards in the Baccarat Sector.(37) Its Infantry rifle strength on this date was about 12,800. (38) The frontage strength per hundred yards would therefore be about 69 Infantry rifles. The Baccarat Sector, while in the western Vosges, might be involved in any major operation on the favorable ground around Nancy. At this date, however, major operations were in progress much farther west.

On August 23, 1918, the 89th Division held a front of about 175 hundred yards in the Lucey Sector.(39) Its Infantry rifle strength on this date was about 12,000.(40) The frontage strength per hundred yards would therefore be about 68 Infantry rifles. The Lucey Sector was in the Woevre, where the front had been inactive for years, and the thickening of the line for the St. Mihiel operations was delayed beyond this date to secure the effect of surprise.(41)

On August 24, 1918, the 29th Division held a front of about 155 hundred yards east of Belfort.(42) Its Infantry rifle strength on this date was about 12,800.(43) The frontage strength per hundred yards would therefore be about 83 Infantry rifles. While major operations would be possible through the Belfort gap, the need for troops in the battle raging in the north assured that this would remain a quiet sector.

The average frontage strength in the four instances given is, for every hundred yards, 64 Infantry rifles. This can be taken as approximating the normal. Figures drawn from other instances might materially modify the average given, but the instances cited are believed to be normal, while many other occupations which might have been cited might be abnormal and based on convenience. For example, on August 16, 1918, the 1st Division held a front of about 115 hundred yards, in the Saizerais Sector.(44) Its Infantry rifle strength on this date was about 13,000.(45) The frontage strength per hundred yards would therefore be 113 Infantry rifles. The division held nearly twice as powerfully as the 89th Division on its immediate left. No reason is apparent for this condition other than convenience. The division held this sector for only a few weeks between two major operations and it was convenient to have it take over the exact sector of the weaker French division it relieved.

Map furnished by 1st Div., Aug. 16, 1918. Map room files G-3, A. E. F. (44)
1st Div. Returns for July and August, 1918. Files of A. G. O. (45)

### 5. American Occupation of an Active Front.

On June 4, 1918, the 1st Division held a front of about 76 hundred yards in the Cantigny Sector.(46) Its Infantry rifle strength on this date was about 13,000.(47) The frontage strength per hundred yards would therefore be about 171 Infantry rifles. At this date a German major offensive was imminently expected on this front, and the Artillery preparation for the German offensive from Montdidier to Noyon on June 9, 1918, actually included this front.

Map furnished by 1st Div., June 4, 1918. Map room files G-3, A. E. F. (46)
1st Div. Returns for May and June, 1918. Files A. G. O. File 48, H. B. (47)

On August 16, 1918, the 3d Corps held a front of about 120 hundred yards at Fismes on the Vesle. It had in line the 28th and 77th Divisions(48) with an Infantry rifle strength of approximately 21,000.(49) The frontage strength per hundred yards would therefore be about 175 Infantry rifles. The advance to the Vesle had just been completed and this front was held against possible strong reaction and preliminary to an offensive from the Vesle.(50)

Official map of American front of Aug. 16, 1918. Map room files G-3, A. E. F.
F. O. 13, 3d Army Corps, Aug. 12, 1918. H. B. 183-2. (48)
28th and 77th Div. Returns for July and Aug. 1918. Files of A. G. O. (49)
Rept. of C. in C., A. E. F., cabled Nov. 20, 1918, p. 12. (50)

On September 21, 1918, the 78th Division held a front of about 76 hundred yards northeast of Thiaucourt.(51) Its Infantry rifle strength on this date was about 12,300. (52) The frontage strength per hundred yards would

The Tactical Operations of the 78th Div., A.E.F. quoting F. O. 3 4th A. C., Sept 21, 1918. H.

the 2d and 5th Divisions after the St. Mihiel operation and was holding the front against possible strong reaction.

<small>Weekly Graphics of Personnel, Sept. 25, 1918. Files G-1, A.E.F. (52)</small>

The average frontage strength per hundred yards in the instances given, covering four divisions, was 171 Infantry rifles. This can be accepted as approximating the normal. There were not many cases of the occupation of an active front by American divisions except when engaged in major operations.

### 6. American Participation in a Major Operation.

On July 18, 1918, the 1st Division attacked on a front of about 29 hundred yards south of Soissons.(53) Its Infantry rifle strength on this date was approximately 13,500.(54) The frontage strength per hundred yards would be about 465 Infantry rifles.

<small>F. O. 27, 1st Div., July 16, 1918. H.B.201-13. (53)
1st Div. Returns for June and July, 1918. Files of A. G. O. (54)</small>

On September 12, 1918, the 5th Division attacked on a front of about 25 hundred yards in the St. Mihiel operation.(55) Its Infantry rifle strength on this date was approximately 12,900.(56) The frontage strength per hundred yards would be about 516 Infantry rifles. It should be noted here that this is the greatest strength that will appear in this study. The following conditions appear to have produced it: The division was attacking through comparatively open ground in the center of the main attack of the First Army. This explains why its strength per unit of front is the maximum in the Army, approximately equaled by the 2d and 42d Divisions, which attacked under similar circumstances, but greater than that of the 89th, also a center division, but facing a solid mass of woods, where progress should be slower and the need of original impulse consequently less.(57) Success in this operation was of prime importance, and the First Army had ample reserve divisions which could have been used to thicken the line if necessary.(58) It, therefore, appears that the strength per unit of front shown by the 5th Division was the greatest economically desirable in a major operation. The instance can, however, be fairly cited in arriving at the frontage strength in a major operation, as only center divisions are wholly committed to the operation as such. Against this figure should be noted, however, the frontage strength on the whole front of the southern St. Mihiel attack. The 1st and 4th Corps, with seven divisions in line, had about 89,000 Infantry

<small>F. O. 41, 5th Division, Sept. 9, 1918. H. B. 205-5. (55)
Weekly Graphics of Personnel, Sept. 25, 1918. Files G-1, A.E.F. Skeleton 5th Div. History, G-3 files, A.E.F. (56)
Official map of St. Mihiel Offensive. Map room files G-3, A.E.F.
Report of C. G., 1st Army, G-3 files, A.E.F. (57)
Rept. of C. in C., A. E. F., cabled Nov. 20, 1918, pp. 14-15. (58)
Map of St. Mihiel Offensive. Map room files G-3, A.E.F.
Rept. of C in C., A. E. F., cabled Nov. 20, 1918, pp. 13-14.</small>

rifles on a front of about 380 hundred yards. (59) The frontage strength per hundred yards would be about 235 Infantry rifles over the whole front of these two corps.

On September 26, 1918, the 5th Corps attacked in the center of the First Army attack on a front of about 115 hundred yards between the Meuse River and the Argonne Forest. It had the 79th, 37th, and 91st Divisions in line (60) with an Infantry rifle strength of about 37,000. (61) The frontage strength per hundred yards would be about 321 Infantry rifles.

On October 17, 1918, the 2d Corps attacked as a part of the Fourth British Army on a front of about 40 hundred yards south of Le Cateau. It had the 27th and 30th Divisions in line (62), with an Infantry rifle strength of about 16,300. (63) The frontage strength per hundred yards would be about 408 Infantry rifles. The average frontage strength per hundred yards in the instances given, covering seven divisions, was about 394 Infantry rifles. This can be accepted as approximately normal, and conforms to British and French statements as to best practices. (64)

Weekly Graphics of Personnel. Sept. 25, 1918. G-1 files, A. E. F. (59)

Official map Meuse-Argonne Offensive. Map room files G-3, A. E. F.
Rept. C. in C. A. E. F., cabled Nov. 20, 1918, p. 16. (60)
Weekly Graphics of Personnel, Oct. 2, 1918. Files G-1, A. E. F. (61)

2d Army Corps Instructions, Series B, No. 1. Preliminary order Oct. 14, 1918. H. B. 182–8. (62)
Weekly Graphics of Personnel, Oct. 23, 1918. Files G-1, A.E.F. (63)

The Division in Attack. 88–135, Nov., 1918. General Staff College Library.
Instructions on the Defensive Action of Large Units in Battle. W. D. D. 784, 1918. (64)

### 7. American Participation in Open Warfare.

On November 11, 1918, the 3d Corps was attacking in the First Army on a front of about 295 hundred yards east of the Meuse. It had in line the 32d, 5th, and 90th Divisions, (65) with an Infantry rifle strength of about 25,000. (66) The frontage strength per hundred yards was about 85 Infantry rifles.

On the same date and under the same command, the 5th Corps was attacking on a front of about 200 hundred yards in an operation involving crossing the Meuse. It had in line the 89th and 2d Divisions, (67) with a rifle strength of about 18,000. (68) The frontage strength per hundred yards would be about 90 Infantry rifles.

The average frontage strength per hundred yards in the instances given, covering five divisions, was 87 Infantry rifles. This may be taken as not abnormal, even if not deduced from long experience. Warfare in the battle between the Meuse and the Argonne gradually changed character from assault on an elaborately organized position on September 26 to practically open war on November 11. It is from the last date, therefore, that instances are taken.

F. O. 57, 2d Army Corps, Nov. 10, 1918. H. B. 183–2.
Map of Meuse-Argonne Offensive. Map room files G-3, A. E. F. (65)
Weekly Graphics of Personnel, Nov. 20, 1918. Files G-1, A.E.F. (66)
Map of Meuse-Argonne Offensive. Map room files G-3, A. E. F.
Rept. C. in C. A. E. F., cabled Nov. 20, 1918, p. 21. (67)
Weekly Graphics of Personnel, Nov. 13, 1918. Files G-1, A. E. F. (68)

It must be borne in mind that attack was not necessarily continuous along the front of a division, and that the map even shows definitely that the line was not continuous. An advance by column on a narrow front instanced by the 2d Division on November 3d might pull forward the entire Army front. These figures show an interesting and abrupt change from the frontage strength of major operations, from which open warfare may swiftly materialize. Corroborated by French and British experience, they indicate that the dense massing of troops, made possible by stabilization of a front, is forbidden in open warfare by difficulties attendant on troop movement, supply, and communication.(69)

<small>Features of the War. Haig, p. 12. (69)</small>

### 8. General Discussion of French and British Practices.

It would be misleading to attempt to compute French and British practices from specific instances. Documents giving such instances are generally only available owing to association of our units with foreign units, and are too infrequently available to warrant drawing general conclusions and data therefrom. General statements as to practices are found in studies on the number of troops to the yard in principal battles during the last half of the nineteenth century and deductions drawn therefrom by foreign authorities.(70) These practices are more or less confirmed, and at any rate brought up to date, in instructions issued by French and British military authorities toward the end of the war with Germany, which give the desirable practices in certain instances.(71) The specific instances given below are only of value as showing a tendency to maintain the attacking or defending strength prescribed in the instruction pamphlets, as determined by the general experiences of the French and British armies on the western front. Very general and valuable information is afforded by copies of French Allied Order of Battle Maps, but information as to actual British occupations is less satisfactory.

<small>Memorandum on Number of Troops to the Yard in the Principal Battles since 1850. General Staff College Library. (70)</small>

<small>Instructions on the Defensive Action of Large Units in Battle. W. D. D. 794, 1918. The Division in Attack. 88–135, Nov., 1918. General Staff College Library. (71)</small>

### 9. French and British Occupation of a Quiet Front.

On June 25, 1916, the French Group of Armies of the East held a front of about 2,900 hundred yards from St. Mihiel to the Swiss border, with 18 divisions in line.(72) No exact data as to the strength of these divisions are available. Divisional strengths varied considerably. This was about the time of the change in organization of

<small>Copy of French Official Order of Battle Map for June 25, 1916. Map room files G-3, A. E. F. (72)</small>

French divisions.(73) The strength is therefore taken as 6,880 Infantry rifles per division, the full strength in the new organization. The strength of the 18 divisions would be about 143,840 Infantry rifles. The frontage strength per hundred yards would be about 49 Infantry rifles. Statement of Lieut. Col. de Chambrun, French Army, Nov. 14, 1918. (73)

On October 13, 1918, the same Group of Armies held a front of about 2,100 hundred yards from Nomeny to the Swiss border, with 12 French and 3 American, or the equivalent of 18 French divisions, in line.(74) At divisional strengths given in Gen. Pershing's cablegram of May 11, 1918, the rifle strength would be about 121,500. The frontage strength per hundred yards would be 58 Infantry rifles. Copy of French Official Order of Battle Map, Oct. 13, 1918. Map room files G-3, A. E. F. (74)

The average for the two cases cited would be 54 Infantry rifles per hundred yards. This does not vary too much from cases of exceptional extension in preceding wars, which have fallen as low as 80 Infantry rifles per hundred yards for defending troops.(75) Nor does the French figure materially differ from that of American divisions on similar fronts, which has been seen to be about 64 Infantry rifles per hundred yards. Memorandum on Number of Troops to the Yard in the Principal Battles since 1850. General Staff College Library (75).

On November 11, 1917, the British Third Army held a front of about 600 hundred yards in front of Cambrai, with 11 divisions in line.(76) No exact figures on the strength of these divisions are available. Before Gen. Byng's tank attack the Cambrai front was regarded as being as quiet a sector as any in the British zone, and the map shows that it was lightly held in comparison to the rest of the British front. The holding divisions can therefore be taken as depleted to a rifle strength of about 9,000 each or the average for the early spring of 1918. The Army rifle strength would be about 99,000. The frontage strength per hundred yards would be about 165 Infantry rifles. It will be noted that this is a much larger figure than that found in the case of American and French occupations. The discrepancy is probably explained by the fact that on no part of the British front were major operations so unlikely, on account of difficulties of terrain, as in the Vosges Sector, from which American and French instances have been taken. Copy of French Official Order of Battle Map for Nov. 11, 1917. Map room files G-3, A. E. F. (76)

**10. French and British Occupation of an Active Front.**

On August 23, 1916, the French Second Army held a front of about 850 hundred yards around Verdun, with 17 divisions in line.(77) It has been seen that French Copy of French Official Order of Battle Map for Aug. 23, 1916. Map room files G-3, A. E. F. (77)

divisions had recently been reduced to three Infantry regiments; the full strength of the new organization is therefore taken, or 6,880 Infantry rifles. This gives a total for the Army of about 116,960 Infantry rifles. The frontage strength per hundred yards would be about 137 Infantry rifles, which can be accepted as not abnormal. On the date in question the German assault had been worn out (78) and the front may be considered as merely very active. Despite the statement in French instructions that divisional fronts depend on varying conditions, and that there is no average or theoretical front, French military authorities give an approximate front for a division engaged in actual defensive battle in 1918 as from 22 to 44 hundred yards. (79) Assuming that the lesser density may be taken, on a front where battle is merely expected, the frontage strength per hundred yards would be 153 Infantry rifles. This agrees nearly enough to confirm, as of value, the factor of 137 found in the case of the French Second Army.

<small>History of the World War. Simonds. Vol. III. (78)</small>

<small>Instructions on the Defensive Action of Large Units in Battle. W. D. D. 794, 1918. (79)</small>

On March 17, 1918, the British Third Army held a front of about 430 hundred yards in the vicinity of Arras, with 10 divisions in line. (80) It has been seen that before this date British divisions were reduced to 9 battalions. The strength of the 10 divisions would therefore be 90,000 Infantry rifles at the maximum. The frontage strength per hundred yards would be 210 Infantry rifles at the maximum.

<small>Map of Mar. 17, 1918. British Situation Maps, D-1. Map room files G-3, A. E. F. (80)</small>

### 11. French and British Participation in a Major Operation.

On August 10, 1918, the French First Army was attacking, in conjunction with the attack of the British Fourth Army, on a front of about 300 hundred yards in the vicinity of Montdidier. It had 10 divisions in the front line, (81) which at the strength which has been accepted from May, 1918, give a rifle strength of about 67,500. The frontage strength per hundred yards would be 227 Infantry rifles.

<small>Copy of French Official Order of Battle Map for Aug. 10, 1918. Map room files G-3, A. E. F. (81)</small>

It will be noted that despite the fact that this attack was one of the most successful of the war, the frontage strength is very much smaller than that determined for individual American divisions in similar attacks, such as that of the 5th Division at St. Mihiel. However, the density is naturally reduced in figuring from the large front and strength of an army, by the inclusion of divisions on the flank of the attack which may not be actually assaulting on the day in question, and consequently are in lesser density. It will be remembered that while the frontage strength of the 5th Division at St. Mihiel was 516 Infantry rifles, the frontage strength computed for the whole southern attack was only 235 Infantry rifles per hundred yards. The French figure approaches, however, the maximum density of 306 Infantry rifles per hundred yards for a division engaged in defensive battle, obtained from the French instructions cited in the preceding numbered paragraph. The maximum density under such circumstances may be accepted as approximately the proper density for a division on favorable ground in the center of a major offensive.

An example of what may be considered the greatest density desirable under the circumstances may be obtained from the following incident: Gen. Petain gave Gen. Fayolle, commanding the Group of Armies of the Reserve, 12 divisions for the attack of July 18, 1918, south of Soissons. Later Gen. Petain asked if one of these divisions could be spared. Gen. Fayolle answered that it could, as his original plan had called for one division to attack in the valley of the Aisne, but that it was not vital to attack on this part of the front.(82) It may be assumed that had Gen. Fayolle wished greater density on the front on which he actually attacked, he would have used this division to attain it. The frontage strength per hundred yards of front for the 1st Division in this attack has been seen to have been 465 Infantry rifles. The French divisions, weaker in Infantry rifles, attacked on a narrower front.(83) The density found for the 1st Division can therefore be accepted as approximately the maximum desirable under the circumstances in the opinion of the French high command.

Statement of Lieut. Col. de Chambrun, French Army, Nov. 14, 1918. (82)

Statement of Lieut. Col. de Chambrun, French Army, Nov. 14, 1918. (83)

On August 10, 1918, the British Fourth Army was attacking on a front of about 370 hundred yards east of Amiens. It had 9 British and 1 American divisions in line.(84) The American division can be taken at approximately full strength, or 13,500 Infantry rifles. If the British divisions be taken as approximately one-half of this, on the authority given above, the Army would have in line 74,250 Infantry rifles. The frontage strength per hundred yards would be about 200 Infantry rifles. The same remarks as to the success of the operation and as to density made in the case of the French First Army

Copy of French Official Order of Battle Map, Aug. 10, 1918. Map room files G-3, A. E. F. (84)

engaged in the same attack apply here. However, the frontage strength found for the British Fourth Army approaches the figure of best practices given in British military instructions in 1918. These give a frontage strength as varying from 100 men per hundred yards of front upward for a division in the attack, but state that a smaller density than 300 to 500 per hundred yards will rarely prove successful.(85)

<small>The Division in Attack. 88–135. General Staff College Library. (85)</small>

The frontage strengths so far developed in the study of major operations during the war with Germany are considerably less than those given by the best authorities before the war with Germany as desirable strengths for attack.(86) It is evident that this was not caused by the shortage of men on such a large front, as there is a general agreement between American, British, and French authorities, fixing the density desirable in an attack as about 300 to 500 men per hundred yards. The smaller density found desirable in this last war is probably the direct result of the highly developed power of modern artillery and machine guns.

<small>Memorandum on Number of Troops to the Yard in the Principal Battles since 1850. General Staff College Library. (86)</small>

### 12. French and British Participation in Open Warfare.

On September 27, 1914, the French forces were deployed on a front of about 5,400 hundred yards. This excludes a small front held by the British Expeditionary Corps. The French occupation extended from Douai to about 80 kilometers north of the Swiss border, and included about 43 divisions in line.(87) The average strength in Infantry rifles was not at this time above 12,000 per division. It may have been less.(88) At the maximum there is obtained the frontage strength per hundred yards of 95 Infantry rifles. Not only is this figure obtained from very incomplete data, it manifestly does not even represent the strength in which the portions of the front actually were held. The map shows frequent large gaps between units. The figure is, however, of value as confirming the inevitability shown in American instances of employing in open warfare a less density per unit of front along the whole front of operations than in major operations on the stabilized line.

<small>Copy of French Official Order of Battle Map for Sept. 27, 1914. Map room files G-3, A.E.F. (87)

Statement of Lieut. Col. de Chambrun, French Army, Nov. 14, 1918. (88)</small>

A study of modern warfare previous to the war with Germany, with the fighting on a stabilized line that it developed, shows frontage strengths very much larger than those found for American and French units. The

<small>Memorandum on Number of Troops to the Yard in the Principal Battles since 1850. General Staff College Library. (89)</small>

strengths in previous wars are, however, figured merely from the front on which battle was actually engaged, without considering at all the rest of the field of operations. (89) In spite, therefore, of the apparent density of troops in previous modern wars, it appears that a maximum density on large fronts was developed in the great attacks of the war with Germany.

The experience of the British Expeditionary Corps in 1914 was too chaotic and changing even to attempt to draw therefrom any British frontage strength in open warfare. The British forces naturally had the same experience in semi-open warfare in the days preceding the armistice as did the American Expeditionary Forces. On November 10, 1918, the British First and Third Armies, with 14 divisions in line, were advancing on a front of about 715 hundred yards in the region of Mons. (90) At a divisional rifle strength of about 6,000, the frontage strength per hundred yards would be about 120 Infantry rifles.

<sub>Combined Order of Battle Map, Nov. 10, 1918. Map room files G-3, A.E.F. (90)</sub>

### 13. Conclusions.

Conclusions drawn from this study are summarized in a table which follows. It must be consulted, however, with these facts in mind: In an effort to give a simple tabulation round numbers only have been employed. In cases where a statement of best practices has been found, that statement has been adopted rather than figures drawn from isolated instances. The frontage strengths in open warfare are figured on the entire front of the operation. The very name "open warfare" indicates the condition that exists. Troops operate as units, with open spaces between them. The frontage strength of a division or smaller unit would therefore be much denser if figured on the front physically occupied by that unit. So figured, it would depend on the formation adopted. This formation might very well approximate and give the same frontage strength as the formation of a division or smaller unit in a major operation on a stabilized front. The considerations which dictate both formations are the same—the necessity for obtaining maximum power and the desirability of minimizing losses.

*Best practices in the number of Infantry rifles employed per hundred yards of front.*

[In round numbers.]

|  | American. | French. | British. |
|---|---|---|---|
| Quiet front | 60 | 50 | 160 |
| Active front | 170 | 150 | 210 |
| Major operation | 400 | 310 | 400 |
| Open warfare | 90 | 90 | 120 |

### 14. Proportion of Divisional, Corps, and Army Troops to Infantry Rifles.

For the purposes of this study the unit of strength has been taken as the number of Infantry rifles in front line divisions. The number of Infantry rifles for a unit of front under varying conditions has been determined. Consideration of other divisional troops and corps and army troops has been omitted in order to clarify this discussion. With the basic figures established, however, a consideration of the proper proportion of other divisional troops and of corps and army troops is interesting.

<small>Deductions from the World War. Von Freytag-Loringhoven, p. 129. (91)</small>

No organization can cover all the possible contingencies of modern war.(91) The great war abundantly proved this. To attempt to deduce proper proportions from prewar European organization and the changes made would be bewildering. Fortunately there exists a statement of best practices in the organization of a field army with Service of Supply troops in the Priority Schedule prepared at General Headquarters, A. E. F. This is supplemented by Tables of Organization, 1918, sufficiently to determine proportions without reference to the million and one varying instances which might be selected from the war experience of American, French, and British troops.

<small>Report of C. in C., A. E. F., cabled Nov. 20, 1919, pp. 1-3. (92)</small>

<small>Confidential cable No. 876, A. E. F., Apr. 9, 1918. (93)</small>

<small>Report of Commanding General, First Army, A. E. F., pp. 128-129, 132-133. (94)</small>

The two documents cited above were prepared after a thorough consideration of allied organization and experience after years of war.(92) They may therefore fairly be assumed to represent a composition of the best practices of allied armies. The Priority Schedule was not completely followed as drawn up, owing principally to the urgent necessity for shipment of Infantry and machine-gun units to meet the emergencies of the spring of 1918.(93) The essential soundness of division and corps organization was proved in the experience of the First American Army.(94)

It should be noted that aviation units were not figured in the Priority Schedule. Aviation was given a separate schedule without regard for maintaining a properly balanced army in an effort to lend most rapid assistance to the allied cause.(95) As it was omitted from the proportions arrived at by Gen. Pershing, it may be omitted in arriving at the proper proportions desired for this study, merely bearing in mind that an inclusion of aviation would increase the proportion of corps, army, and S. O. S. troops.

<small>Letter from C. in C., A. E. F., Oct. 7, 1917. H. B. 45-7.(95)</small>

Another point which must be considered is the inclusion of replacement divisions in S. O. S. troops. While originally included in the organization of corps,(96) replacement divisions actually seldom functioned as such within the corps, and replacements were drawn from the general reservoir of newly arrived divisions.(97) Best authorities give the proper basis for number of divisions actually functioning within a corps as four, two in line and two in reserve.(98) Replacement divisions are consequently figured in S. O. S. totals.

<small>T. of O., Series B, Table 101, 1918.(96)</small>
<small>Report of C. in C., A. E. F., cabled Nov. 20, 1918, pp. 17 and 23.(97)</small>
<small>Report of C. in C., A. E. F., cabled Nov. 20, 1918, p. 3. Report of C. G., First Army, pp. 132-133. (98)</small>

A third question to be decided is the number of corps in an army which would normally be in line. The First Army generally employed four corps in the attack in the Meuse-Argonne battle, three west of the river, one east. (99) While other corps in the First Army were under the circumstances actually employed in line, the Army commander in his report insists on the necessity of a corps in reserve.(100) While the ideal corps in this report is described as without permanently assigned divisions (101), there were always divisions in Army reserve which could have been administered by such a corps. The fifth corps included in the Priority Schedule is therefore considered as being, with its combat divisions, in Army reserve.

<small>Report of C. G., First Army, pp. 102 et seq. (99)</small>
<small>Id., pp. 10. (100)</small>
<small>Id., pp. 132-133. (101)</small>

The number of Infantry rifles in a division is 13,568; the total number of officers and men is 28,172.(102) For the purposes of the Priority Schedule, however, the division was taken at 27,063.(103) In order to tie the number of rifles into the Priority Schedule, the latter figure is used in obtaining proportions. The number of Infantry rifles is 50 per cent of the strength of the division.

<small>T. of O., Series A, 1918, Tables 1 and 3. (102)</small>
<small>Priority Schedule, G-3 files, A. E. F., p. 7. (103)</small>

The number of Infantry rifles on the front of a typical corps with two divisions in line is 27,136. The total number of officers and men in the typical corps is 177,070; less 2 replacement divisions, it is 122,944.(104) The number of Infantry rifles on the corps front is therefore 22 per cent of the corps strength in the corps sector.

The number of Infantry rifles on the front of a typical army with four corps in line, each with 2 divisions in line, is 108,544. The total number of officers and men in the typical army of five typical corps, plus army troops, is 685,214. The number of Infantry rifles on the army front is therefore 16 per cent of the army strength. It is 9 per cent of the strength of the army and the necessary S. O. S. troops for its supply, including replacement divisions.(105)

## STATEMENT OF WORKS, DOCUMENTS, AND PERSONS CONSULTED (IN ORDER OF CITATION).

Features of the War. Haig. W. D. D. 952, 1919.
Deductions from the World War. Von Freytag-Loringhoven.
The War of Positions. Azan.
Memorandum on Number of Troops to the Yard in the Principal Battles since 1850. U 167-G 74. General Staff College Library.
Strength and Organization of the Armies of France, etc. W. D. D. 22, 1916.
Changes in Organization Found Necessary during the Progress of the European War. W. C. D. 4886-23, 1915.
Confidential Cablegrams, A. E. F., 1917-18.
Brig. Gen. George Simonds, Chief of Staff, 2d Corps.
British Situation Maps, map room files G-3, A. E. F.
Report of C. in C., A. E. F., cabled Nov. 20, 1918.
The War with Germany. Ayers.
Instructions on the Offensive Action of Large Units in Battle. No. 767, Headquarters, A. E. F., 1918. (Translation from French document.)
Instructions on the Defensive Action of Large Units in Battle. W. D. D. 794, 1918. (Translation from French document.)
Tables of Organization, Series A and B, 1918.
Field Orders, 1st Division, Historical Branch, file 201.
Tableaux d'Effectifs. U. A. 702-A 39 (1913-18). General Staff College Library.
London Times History of the War.
Lieut. Col. de Chambrun, French Army, attached to Gen. Pershing's Staff.
History of the World War. Simonds.
Field Orders, 2d Division, Historical Branch, file 202.
Divisional Maps, map room files G-3, A. E. F.
Divisional Returns, files A. G. O.
Maps of American Fronts, map room files G-3, A. E. F.
Field Orders, 3d Army Corps, Historical Branch, file 183-2.
The Tactical Operations of the 78th Division, Historical Branch, file 278.
Weekly Graphics of Personnel, files G-1, A. E. F.
Field Orders, 5th Division, Historical Branch, file 205.
Skeleton 5th Division History, files G-3, A. E. F.
Report of Commanding General, First Army, files G-3, A. E. F.
Second Army Corps Instructions, Historical Branch, files 182.
The Division in Attack, SS-135, Nov., 1918. General Staff College Library.
Copies of French Official Order of Battle Maps, map room files G-3, A. E. F.
Combined Order of Battle Maps, map room files, G-3, A. E. F.
Letter from C. in C., A. E. F., Oct. 7, 1917. Historical Branch, file 45-7.
Priority Schedule, files G-3, A. E. F.

Printed by Libri Plureos GmbH in Hamburg,
Germany